CH00738990

PAW-PAW LEAVES RECIPES

A comprehensive guide to the Treatment of all types of cancer and digestion

Julie Winston

Copyright © (Julie Winston) 2023. All rights reserved

Paw-paw leaves Recipes

A comprehensive guide to the treatment
of all types of cancer and digestion

Julie winston

Table of contents

Acknowledgments

Writing a comprehensive guide on culinary creativity with paw-paw leaves has been a delightful journey, and it wouldn't have been possible without the support, inspiration, and contributions of many individuals and resources.

I would like to extend my heartfelt gratitude to:

- Family and Friends: Your unwavering encouragement and willingness to be my taste testers during countless experiments are deeply appreciated. Thank you for your enthusiasm and patience.

- Culinary Mentors: To those who have shared their culinary wisdom, thank you for nurturing my passion for cooking and inspiring the creation of this guide.

- Farmers and Gardeners: A special thank you to those who cultivate paw-paw trees and graciously share their knowledge of caring for these unique plants.

- Botanists and Biologists: Your insights into the world of paw-paw leaves have been invaluable in providing accurate and relevant information.

- Readers and Enthusiasts: To all those who embark on this culinary journey, I extend my heartfelt thanks. Your curiosity and desire to explore the culinary world of paw-paw leaves drive my passion for sharing this knowledge.

- Nature: The source of inspiration and nourishment for all culinary adventures. Thank you for providing the ingredients we cherish and enjoy.

- The Written Word: To the authors and scholars whose work has provided a foundation for this guide, thank you for your dedication to sharing knowledge.

This project has been a labor of love, and I am deeply grateful to every individual and resource that has contributed to its creation. Your support, encouragement, and expertise have been instrumental in bringing this guide to life.

With warm regards,

[Julie Winston]

Dedication

This book is dedicated to those who find joy in the art of cooking and the magic of creativity in the kitchen. To the passionate home chefs, culinary explorers, and all those who believe that every meal can be a delightful adventure, this book is for you.

May you continue to savor the flavors of life, experiment with enthusiasm, and relish the unique and diverse world of culinary possibilities that surrounds us.

Thank you for your love of food, your boundless curiosity, and your commitment to the culinary arts.

With heartfelt appreciation,

[Julie Winston]

Chapter 1: Introduction

About Paw-Paw Leaves

Paw-paw leaves, scientifically known as "Carica papaya," are an often underappreciated natural wonder. These leaves come from the paw-paw tree, a tropical fruit tree that is native to Central America but has found its way to many parts of the world. Paw-paw leaves have gained recognition not only for their culinary potential but also for their remarkable health benefits.

The Paw-Paw Tree

The paw-paw tree is a small, evergreen tree that typically reaches a height of 10 to 30 feet. It is most famous for its sweet and delicious fruit, the paw-paw, but its leaves also play a significant role in various traditional cuisines and natural remedies. The tree's distinct tropical appearance and wide, vibrant leaves make it easy to spot in its natural habitat.

A Culinary Secret

The culinary use of paw-paw leaves is a well-kept secret in many regions. These leaves have a unique flavor profile, often described as slightly bitter and peppery with a hint of nuttiness. They can be incorporated into a wide range of dishes, from soups and stews to desserts and beverages, lending their distinctive taste to each creation.

Health Benefits

Paw-paw leaves are not only delicious but also packed with health-promoting compounds. It's no wonder they have been revered for their medicinal properties for centuries. Here are some of the key health benefits associated with paw-paw leaves:

1. Nutrient-Rich Powerhouse

Paw-paw leaves are a rich source of essential vitamins and minerals, including vitamins A, C, E, and B vitamins, as well as minerals like calcium, magnesium, and iron. These nutrients are crucial for maintaining overall health.

2. Antioxidant Properties

These leaves are loaded with antioxidants, such as flavonoids, which help protect your body from oxidative stress and reduce the risk of chronic diseases.

3. Anti-Inflammatory Effects

Paw-paw leaves contain compounds that possess anti-inflammatory properties, making them valuable for those with inflammatory conditions or looking to reduce inflammation in the body.

4. Immune Boosting

The high vitamin C content in paw-paw leaves can boost your immune system, helping your body fend off infections and illnesses.

5. Digestive Aid

Traditionally, paw-paw leaves have been used to aid digestion. They can help relieve digestive discomfort and promote a healthy gut.

6. Blood Sugar Regulation

Some studies suggest that paw-paw leaves may play a role in regulating blood sugar levels, potentially benefiting individuals with diabetes or those at risk of the condition.

7. Skin Health

The topical application of paw-paw leaf extracts may contribute to healthier skin by reducing blemishes and promoting a radiant complexion.

Safety Precautions

While paw-paw leaves offer a host of benefits, it's important to be aware of some safety precautions:

- Quality Matters: Ensure that you use fresh, healthy leaves from a trusted source, free from pesticides or other contaminants.

- Moderation: As with any ingredient, moderation is key. Avoid excessive consumption of paw-paw leaves, as it may lead to digestive discomfort in some individuals.

- Allergies: Be mindful of potential allergies or sensitivities to paw-paw leaves. It's advisable to try a small amount first if you're unsure.

This introductory chapter provides a comprehensive overview of paw-paw leaves, covering their culinary potential and numerous health benefits, while also emphasizing safety considerations for their use in cooking and natural remedies.

Chapter 2: Gathering and Preparing Paw-Paw Leaves

Paw-paw leaves are a versatile ingredient, but to harness their full potential, it's crucial to know how to properly gather and prepare them. In this chapter, we'll delve into the art of collecting these leaves and ensuring they're ready for use in your culinary creations.

Harvesting Tips

1. Choose Healthy Leaves: When harvesting paw-paw leaves, look for vibrant, healthy leaves free from signs of disease or pests. The best leaves are typically young and

tender, as they tend to have a milder flavor.

2. Timing Matters: The best time to harvest paw-paw leaves is in the morning when the leaves are still fresh and filled with moisture. Avoid harvesting during or after rain, as this can dilute the flavor.

3. Prune Gently: To harvest paw-paw leaves, use clean and sharp pruning shears or scissors. Carefully snip the leaves from the tree, ensuring you don't damage the surrounding branches or the tree's overall health.

4. Leave Some Behind: It's important to be mindful of the tree's well-being. Avoid over-harvesting; leave a reasonable amount of leaves on the tree to

allow it to continue to grow and thrive.

Cleaning and Storing

1. Rinse Thoroughly: Once you've harvested the paw-paw leaves, it's essential to rinse them thoroughly under cold running water. This removes any dirt, insects, or debris that may be clinging to the leaves.

2. Pat Dry: After rinsing, gently pat the leaves dry with a clean kitchen towel or paper towel. Avoid vigorous drying, as the leaves can be delicate.

3. Storage Options: To keep paw-paw leaves fresh, you have a few options:

- Refrigeration: You can store them in the refrigerator. Place them in a plastic bag or an airtight container with a damp paper towel to maintain their freshness. They should stay fresh for up to a week.
- Freezing: If you want to preserve them for a more extended period, consider blanching the leaves quickly, cooling them in an ice bath, and then freezing them in portions. This can extend their shelf life for several months.

4. Preparation for Use: Before using paw-paw leaves in your recipes, take a moment to inspect them once more. Remove any discolored or damaged portions, as they can affect the taste and appearance of your dishes.

By following these harvesting and preparation tips, you'll be well on your way to making the most of the unique flavor and health benefits that paw-paw leaves have to offer. Whether you're creating a delightful paw-paw leaf salad or crafting a nourishing soup, starting with properly gathered and prepared leaves is the key to success in the kitchen.

Chapter 3: Beverages

In this chapter, we dive into the world of paw-paw leaf-infused beverages. These refreshing and healthful drinks are not only a delightful way to enjoy the unique flavor of paw-paw leaves but also a fantastic means of reaping their numerous health benefits.

Paw-Paw Leaf Tea

Paw-Paw Leaf Tea is a soothing and comforting beverage enjoyed by

many for its distinct taste and potential health-boosting properties. Here's how to prepare it:

Ingredients:
- Fresh paw-paw leaves
- Water

Instructions:
1. Begin by washing the paw-paw leaves thoroughly, ensuring they are free from dirt or impurities.

2. Boil water in a pot or kettle.

3. Place the clean paw-paw leaves in a teapot or a heatproof container.

4. Pour the boiling water over the leaves and allow them to steep for about 5-7 minutes. You can adjust

the steeping time to achieve your preferred level of flavor.

5. After steeping, strain the tea to remove the leaves, and your paw-paw leaf tea is ready to enjoy. You can add honey or lemon for added flavor if desired.

Paw-Paw Leaf Smoothie

Paw-Paw Leaf Smoothie is a delightful and nutritious way to incorporate paw-paw leaves into your daily routine. It's perfect for those who prefer a refreshing, blended drink.

Ingredients:
- Fresh paw-paw leaves
- Ripe pawpaw fruit
-Greek yogurt (or a dairy-free alternative)
- Honey (or another sweetener of your choice)
- Ice cubes

Instructions:
1. Start by cleaning and preparing the paw-paw leaves as discussed in Chapter 2.

2. In a blender, combine the washed paw-paw leaves, ripe paw-paw fruit (peeled and deseeded), a generous scoop of Greek yogurt, a drizzle of honey, and a handful of ice cubes.

3. Blend until you achieve a smooth and creamy consistency. Adjust the

sweetness with honey to suit your taste.

4. Pour your paw-paw leaf smoothie into a glass and enjoy a nutritious and refreshing drink.

Paw-Paw Leaf Infused Water

Paw-Paw Leaf Infused Water is a simple yet elegant way to enjoy the essence of paw-paw leaves. This hydrating beverage is perfect for those who want a mild and refreshing taste.

Ingredients:
- Fresh paw-paw leaves
- Water
- Slices of citrus fruits (like lemon or lime), for added flavor

Instructions:

1. Once again, ensure your paw-paw leaves are clean and free from impurities.

2. Fill a pitcher or glass container with water.

3. Add the cleaned paw-paw leaves and slices of citrus fruits to the water.

4. Allow the mixture to infuse in the refrigerator for a few hours or overnight for the best flavor.

5. Serve your paw-paw leaf-infused water chilled, and enjoy the subtle yet delightful taste of the leaves.

These paw-paw leaf-infused beverages offer a range of flavors and health benefits. Whether you prefer the comforting warmth of paw-paw leaf tea, the creaminess of a paw-paw leaf smoothie, or the subtlety of infused water, these recipes allow you to savor the unique qualities of paw-paw leaves in a refreshing and hydrating way.

Chapter 4: Soups and Stews

Paw-paw leaves add a distinct flavor and a wealth of nutrients to soups and stews, making them a versatile ingredient in culinary creations from various regions. In this chapter, we'll explore how to use paw-paw leaves to elevate your soups and stews to new heights of flavor and nutrition.

Paw-Paw Leaf Soup

Paw-Paw Leaf Soup is a delicacy enjoyed in many cultures, particularly in parts of Africa and Asia. This soup is celebrated for its unique blend of flavors and its potential health benefits. Here's a recipe to get you started:

Ingredients:
- Fresh paw-paw leaves (cleaned and chopped)
- Protein of your choice (chicken, fish, shrimp, or tofu)
- Onions, garlic, and ginger (for flavor)
- Stock or broth (vegetable or chicken)
- Spices (such as chili, curry, or turmeric)
- Salt and pepper to taste
- Coconut milk or cream (optional)

Instructions:
1. Start by sautéing onions, garlic, and ginger in a pot until they're fragrant.

2. Add your protein of choice and cook until it's lightly browned.

3. Pour in the stock or broth and bring the mixture to a simmer.

4. Add spices and seasonings to taste, creating a flavor profile that suits your preference.

5. Finally, gently stir in the cleaned and chopped paw-paw leaves. Let the soup simmer for a few minutes until the leaves are tender and the flavors have melded.

6. For a creamy variation, you can add a swirl of coconut milk or cream just before serving.

Paw-Paw Leaf Stew

Paw-Paw Leaf Stew is another hearty and satisfying dish that incorporates the unique taste of paw-paw leaves. Here's how you can prepare it:

Ingredients:

- Fresh paw-paw leaves (cleaned and chopped)
- A variety of vegetables (carrots, potatoes, bell peppers, etc.)
- Meat or protein (beef, chicken, lamb, or beans for a vegetarian option)
- Onions, garlic, and herbs for flavor
- Tomato sauce or paste
- Spices (such as paprika, cumin, or coriander)
- Stock or broth (vegetable or meat-based)

Instructions:
1. Begin by sautéing onions and garlic in a large pot until they become translucent.

2. Add your choice of protein and brown it to seal in the flavors.

3. Stir in the tomato sauce or paste, followed by your selection of spices and herbs.

4. Add the chopped vegetables and allow them to soften slightly.

5. Pour in the stock or broth and bring the stew to a gentle simmer.

6. Finally, incorporate the cleaned and chopped paw-paw leaves and let the stew simmer until all the ingredients are tender and the flavors are well integrated.

These paw-paw leaf-infused soups and stews offer a symphony of flavors and textures, making them perfect for warming your body and soul on a chilly day. Experiment with different combinations of ingredients and seasonings to create your unique variations and savor the distinctive essence of paw-paw leaves in each spoonful.

Chapter 5: Main Courses

Paw-paw leaves can take center stage in a variety of main course dishes, contributing a distinct flavor and a host of nutrients. In this chapter, we'll explore how to use paw-paw leaves to create hearty and satisfying main course meals that will impress your taste buds and nourish your body.

Paw-Paw Leaf Rice

Paw-paw leaf Rice is a delightful and aromatic dish that incorporates the earthy and slightly peppery notes of paw-paw leaves. Here's how you can prepare it:

Ingredients:
- Fresh paw-paw leaves (cleaned and chopped)
- Rice (white or brown, depending on your preference)
- Onions, garlic, and ginger (for flavor)
- Protein (chicken, shrimp, or tofu)
- Spices and herbs (such as thyme, bay leaves, or curry powder)
- Stock or broth (vegetable or chicken)
- Salt and pepper to taste

Instructions:
1. Start by sautéing onions, garlic, and ginger in a pan until they're fragrant.

2. Add your choice of protein and cook until it's lightly browned.

3. Stir in the rice and spices, toasting them for a minute to enhance their flavors.

4. Pour in the stock or broth, bringing the mixture to a simmer.

5. Gently fold in the cleaned and chopped paw-paw leaves. Allow the rice to cook until it's tender, and the leaves have blended in beautifully.

6. Season with salt and pepper to taste, and your paw-paw leaf rice is ready to serve.

Paw-Paw Leaf Pasta

Paw-Paw Leaf Pasta is a fusion of flavors that brings the rich taste of paw-paw leaves to a classic Italian favorite. Here's a recipe to get you started:

Ingredients:

- Fresh paw-paw leaves (cleaned and chopped)
- Pasta of your choice (spaghetti, fettuccine, or penne)
- Olive oil
- Garlic, onions, and red pepper flakes (for flavor)
- Grated Parmesan cheese (optional)
- Salt and pepper to taste

Instructions:
1. Begin by boiling the pasta according to the package instructions until it's al dente.

2. While the pasta cooks, sauté garlic and onions in a pan with olive oil until they become fragrant.

3. Stir in the cleaned and chopped paw-paw leaves and cook until they wilt and soften.

4. Once the pasta is ready, drain it and add it to the pan with the paw-paw leaves. Toss everything together to combine the flavors.

5. Season with red pepper flakes, salt, and pepper. If desired, sprinkle with grated Parmesan cheese before serving.

These main course dishes showcase the versatility of paw-paw leaves, infusing your meals with a unique and slightly peppery flavor. Feel free to experiment with various proteins and seasonings to create dishes that suit your palate, and relish the subtle yet distinctive taste of paw-paw leaves in your main course creations.

Chapter 6: Side Dishes

Paw-paw leaves can make for exceptional side dishes, adding a touch of unique flavor and nutrition to complement your main courses. In this chapter, we'll explore how to use paw-paw leaves to create delightful and nutritious side dishes that will elevate your meals.

Paw-Paw Leaf Salad

Paw-Paw Leaf Salad is a refreshing and healthful side dish that combines the delicate taste of paw-paw leaves with a medley of vegetables and dressings. Here's how to prepare it:

Ingredients:
- Fresh paw-paw leaves (cleaned and chopped)
- Mixed greens (such as lettuce, spinach, or arugula)
- Cherry tomatoes
- Cucumber
- Red onion
- Dressing of your choice (vinaigrette, balsamic, or lemon-based)
- Nuts or seeds (such as almonds, sunflower seeds, or walnuts)
- Salt and pepper to taste

Instructions:
1. Begin by thoroughly washing and drying the mixed greens.

2. In a large bowl, combine the mixed greens, cherry tomatoes, cucumber, and red onion.

3. Gently fold in the cleaned and chopped paw-paw leaves.

4. Drizzle your preferred dressing over the salad and toss everything together to coat the ingredients evenly.

5. Top the salad with nuts or seeds for added texture and a touch of crunch.

6. Season with salt and pepper to taste, and your paw-paw leaf salad is ready to serve.

Paw-Paw Leaf Stir-Fry

Paw-Paw Leaf Stir-Fry is a flavorful and colorful side dish that pairs paw-paw leaves with a variety of vegetables and seasonings. Here's a recipe to get you started:

Ingredients:
- Fresh paw-paw leaves (cleaned and chopped)
- A selection of colorful vegetables (bell peppers, broccoli, carrots, etc.)
- Garlic and ginger (for flavor)
- Soy sauce or your preferred stir-fry sauce
- Oil (such as sesame or vegetable oil)
- Salt and pepper to taste

Instructions:
1. Heat oil in a large skillet or wok over medium-high heat.

2. Add minced garlic and ginger and sauté until fragrant.

3. Toss in the colorful vegetables and stir-fry until they're tender-crisp.

4. Incorporate the cleaned and chopped paw-paw leaves and stir-fry for a few more minutes until they wilt and become tender.

5. Drizzle with soy sauce or your preferred stir-fry sauce, and continue to stir-fry until everything is well-coated.

6. Season with salt and pepper to taste, and your paw-paw leaf stir-fry is ready to accompany your main course.

These side dishes offer a wonderful balance of flavors and textures, whether you're looking for a fresh and crisp paw-paw leaf salad or a savory and colorful paw-paw leaf stir-fry. Feel free to experiment with different vegetables, dressings, and seasonings to create side dishes that perfectly complement your meals and introduce your taste buds to the unique essence of paw-paw leaves.

Chapter 7: Snacks and Appetizers

Paw-paw leaves can be used to create delicious snacks and appetizers that are perfect for satisfying your cravings or whetting your appetite before the main course. In this chapter, we'll explore how to incorporate paw-paw leaves into these smaller, delectable dishes.

Paw-Paw Leaf Chips

Paw-Paw Leaf Chips is a delightful and healthier alternative to traditional potato chips. They offer a satisfying crunch and a unique flavor. Here's how to prepare them:

Ingredients:

- Fresh paw-paw leaves (cleaned and dried)
- Olive oil or cooking spray
- Seasonings (such as paprika, cayenne, or salt)
- Optional: grated Parmesan cheese for added flavor

Instructions:

1. Preheat your oven to 350°F (175°C).

2. Start by laying out the cleaned and dried paw-paw leaves on a baking sheet.

3. Lightly drizzle the leaves with olive oil or use a cooking spray to coat them evenly.

4. Sprinkle your choice of seasonings over the leaves. For a

cheesy twist, you can also add grated Parmesan.

5. Bake the leaves for about 10-15 minutes or until they become crisp. Keep an eye on them to prevent burning.

6. Once they're done, allow the chips to cool, and they're ready to be enjoyed as a crunchy snack.

Paw-Paw Leaf Dip

Paw-Paw Leaf Dip is a creamy and flavorful appetizer that pairs well with chips, crackers, or fresh vegetables. Here's a recipe to get you started:

Ingredients:

- Fresh paw-paw leaves (cleaned and chopped)
- Greek yogurt or sour cream
- Cream cheese
- Minced garlic
- Lemon juice
- Salt and pepper to taste
- Optional: grated Parmesan cheese for added flavor

Instructions:

1. Begin by placing the chopped paw-paw leaves, Greek yogurt (or sour cream), and cream cheese in a food processor.

2. Add minced garlic and a splash of lemon juice to the mix.

3. Blend everything until you achieve a smooth and creamy consistency.

4. Season the dip with salt and pepper to taste. If desired, you can also stir in grated Parmesan cheese for an extra layer of flavor.

5. Refrigerate the dip for at least an hour before serving, allowing the flavors to meld.

These snacks and appetizers offer a creative and delicious way to enjoy the unique taste of paw-paw leaves. Whether you're indulging in crispy paw-paw leaf chips or dipping into a creamy paw-paw leaf dip, these dishes are perfect for satisfying your taste buds in smaller, bite-sized portions. Feel free to experiment with different seasonings and variations to create snacks and appetizers that suit your preferences.

Chapter 8: Desserts

Desserts with paw-paw leaves may not be the first thing that comes to mind, but they offer a creative and healthful twist to your sweet treats. In this chapter, we'll explore how to incorporate paw-paw leaves into dessert recipes that will satisfy your sweet tooth while adding a unique and nutritious element.

Paw-Paw Leaf Ice Cream

Paw-Paw Leaf Ice Cream is a cool and refreshing dessert that combines the creaminess of ice cream with the subtle flavors of paw-paw leaves. Here's how to make it:

Ingredients:
- Fresh paw-paw leaves (cleaned and finely chopped)
- Heavy cream or coconut milk (for a dairy-free option)
- Sugar or sweetener of your choice
- Egg yolks (optional, for a custard-style ice cream)
- Vanilla extract
- Salt

Instructions:
1. Start by heating the heavy cream or coconut milk in a saucepan until it's just about to simmer. Remove it from the heat.

2. Add the cleaned and finely chopped paw-paw leaves to the warm liquid, cover, and let it steep for about 30 minutes.

3. After steeping, strain the liquid to remove the paw-paw leaves, pressing down to extract as much flavor as possible.

4. In a separate bowl, whisk together sugar (or your choice of sweetener) and egg yolks, if using.

5. Slowly add the infused cream or coconut milk to the sugar and egg yolk mixture, whisking constantly.

6. Return the mixture to the saucepan and gently heat it until it thickens slightly. Do not let it boil.

7. Remove from heat, add vanilla extract and a pinch of salt, and let it cool.

8. Churn the mixture in an ice cream maker according to the manufacturer's instructions.

9. Once churned, transfer the ice cream to a container, cover it, and freeze until it's firm.

10. Serve your paw-paw leaf ice cream in scoops and enjoy a unique and refreshing dessert.

Paw-Paw Leaf Pudding

Paw-Paw Leaf Pudding is a creamy and comforting dessert that incorporates the slightly bitter and nutty flavors of paw-paw leaves. Here's how to make it:

Ingredients:

- Fresh paw-paw leaves (cleaned and finely chopped)
- Milk (dairy or dairy-free alternative)
- Sugar or sweetener of your choice
- Cornstarch
- Vanilla extract
- Optional: grated dark chocolate or cocoa powder for a chocolate twist

Instructions:

1. In a saucepan, combine milk and cleaned, finely chopped paw-paw leaves. Heat the mixture until it's just about to simmer, then remove it from the heat. Let it steep for about 30 minutes.

2. After steeping, strain the liquid to remove the paw-paw leaves.

3. In a separate bowl, whisk together sugar (or your choice of sweetener) and cornstarch.

4. Slowly add the infused milk to the sugar and cornstarch mixture, whisking constantly.

5. Return the mixture to the saucepan and heat it gently until it thickens. Stir in vanilla extract and optional chocolate elements if desired.

6. Once thickened, remove from heat and let it cool.

7. Serve your paw-paw leaf pudding in bowls or glasses, and enjoy a comforting and flavorful dessert.

These dessert recipes offer a unique and delightful way to

experience the distinctive taste of paw-paw leaves in a sweet and satisfying form. Whether you're savoring a scoop of paw-paw leaf ice cream or indulging in a bowl of paw-paw leaf pudding, these creations are sure to satisfy your sweet cravings with a creative and healthful twist. Feel free to customize these recipes to match your flavor preferences and dietary requirements.

Chapter 9: Special Diets

Paw-paw leaves can be a versatile ingredient for a variety of dietary preferences and restrictions. In this chapter, we'll explore how to adapt paw-paw leaf recipes to suit special diets, including vegan, gluten-free, and keto-friendly options.

Vegan Paw-Paw Leaf Recipes

For those following a vegan diet, paw-paw leaves offer a wealth of possibilities. Here are a couple of vegan-friendly recipes:

Vegan Paw-Paw Leaf Soup

Ingredients:
- Fresh paw-paw leaves (cleaned and chopped)
- Vegetable broth
- Onions, garlic, and ginger (for flavor)

- A variety of vegetables (carrots, bell peppers, etc.)
- Coconut milk (for creaminess)
- Spices (such as curry powder, turmeric, and cayenne)
- Salt and pepper to taste

Instructions:
1. Sauté onions, garlic, and ginger in a pot until they become fragrant.

2. Add a variety of vegetables and stir until they're tender-crisp.

3. Stir in the cleaned and chopped paw-paw leaves.

4. Pour in vegetable broth and bring the mixture to a simmer.

5. Add coconut milk for creaminess and season with spices, salt, and pepper.

6. Simmer until the vegetables and paw-paw leaves are tender, and the flavors are well integrated.

Vegan Paw-Paw Leaf Salad

Ingredients:
- Fresh paw-paw leaves (cleaned and chopped)
- Mixed greens
- Cherry tomatoes
- Cucumber
- Red onion
- Vegan dressing of your choice
- Nuts or seeds (such as almonds or sunflower seeds)
- Salt and pepper to taste

Instructions:
1. Combine the cleaned and chopped paw-paw leaves with mixed greens, cherry tomatoes, cucumber, and red onion.

2. Drizzle your choice of vegan dressing over the salad and toss to coat.

3. Top the salad with nuts or seeds for added texture.

4. Season with salt and pepper to taste, and enjoy your vegan paw-paw leaf salad.

Gluten-Free Paw-Paw Leaf Recipes

For those with gluten sensitivities or following a gluten-free diet, paw-paw leaves can be used in recipes like:

Gluten-Free Paw-Paw Leaf Stir-Fry

Ingredients:
- Fresh paw-paw leaves (cleaned and chopped)
- A variety of gluten-free vegetables (bell peppers, broccoli, carrots, etc.)
- Garlic and ginger for flavor

- Gluten-free soy sauce or tamari
- Oil (such as sesame or vegetable oil)
- Salt and pepper to taste

Instructions:
1. Heat oil in a large skillet or wok over medium-high heat.

2. Add minced garlic and ginger and sauté until fragrant.

3. Toss in gluten-free vegetables and stir-fry until they're tender-crisp.

4. Add the cleaned and chopped paw-paw leaves and stir-fry for a few more minutes until they wilt and become tender.

5. Drizzle with gluten-free soy sauce or tamari and continue to

stir-fry until everything is well-coated.

6. Season with salt and pepper to taste, and your gluten-free paw-paw leaf stir-fry is ready to accompany your main course.

Keto-Friendly Paw-Paw Leaf Recipes

For those on a ketogenic (keto) diet, paw-paw leaves can be used creatively in low-carb recipes. Consider:

Keto-Friendly Paw-Paw Leaf Omelette

Ingredients:
- Fresh paw-paw leaves (cleaned and finely chopped)

- Eggs
- Olive oil or butter
-Grated   Parmesan   cheese
(optional)
- Salt and pepper to taste

Instructions:
1. Heat olive oil or butter in a non-stick skillet over medium heat.

2. In a bowl, whisk eggs, and fold in the cleaned and finely chopped paw-paw leaves.

3. Pour the egg mixture into the skillet, ensuring even distribution of the leaves.

4. Cook until the omelette is set, and the edges turn slightly golden.

5. If desired, sprinkle grated Parmesan cheese over the omelet.

6. Season with salt and pepper to taste, fold the omelet in half, and serve your keto-friendly paw-paw leaf omelet.

These adapted paw-paw leaf recipes cater to different dietary needs and preferences. Whether you're following a vegan, gluten-free, or keto diet, you can enjoy the unique flavors and nutritional benefits of paw-paw leaves in a way that suits your lifestyle. Feel free to experiment and adapt these recipes further to meet your specific dietary requirements.

Chapter 10: Culinary Creativity with Paw-Paw Leaves

Paw-paw leaves offer a world of culinary possibilities, and this final chapter is all about encouraging your creativity in the kitchen. Once you've explored the traditional recipes and adaptations, it's time to experiment and develop your unique dishes that feature the remarkable flavors and health benefits of paw-paw leaves.

Fusion Cuisine

Consider incorporating paw-paw leaves into dishes that blend flavors from various culinary traditions. Whether it's a paw-paw leaf curry with a dash of Mediterranean spices or a paw-paw leaf taco with a Latin twist, fusion cuisine allows you to create exciting and unexpected flavor combinations.

Paw-Paw Leaf Pesto

Paw-paw leaves can be a fantastic addition to a traditional pesto recipe. Blend them with basil, garlic, pine nuts, olive oil, and Parmesan cheese to create a unique and vibrant paw-paw leaf pesto. This pesto can be used as a pasta sauce, sandwich spread, or a dip for fresh bread.

Paw-Paw Leaf Wraps

Use paw-paw leaves as an alternative to traditional wraps or tortillas. Wrap your favorite fillings, whether it's grilled vegetables, protein, or other ingredients, in paw-paw leaves. The slightly bitter taste of the leaves can provide an intriguing contrast to the fillings.

Paw-Paw Leaf Infusions

Paw-paw leaves can be infused into a wide range of beverages, not just tea or water. Try adding them to cocktails, smoothies, or even your homemade fruit juices for a unique twist. The infusion can impart a subtle and refreshing flavor that elevates your drinks.

Dessert Experimentation

Desserts can benefit from the addition of paw-paw leaves as well. Consider incorporating them into your favorite dessert recipes, such as cakes, muffins, or even ice creams, to add a slightly nutty and exotic element to your sweets.

Flavorful Experimentation

Don't be afraid to experiment with various spices, seasonings, and herbs when using paw-paw leaves. The combination of paw-paw leaves with different flavors can yield exciting and unexpected results. Try a dash of cinnamon for warmth, a sprinkle of cumin for earthiness, or a pinch of nutmeg for a hint of sweetness.

Creative Presentation

Enhance the visual appeal of your dishes by getting creative with how you present them. Garnish your paw-paw leaf creations with colorful vegetables, edible flowers, or other visually pleasing elements. A beautifully presented dish can elevate the dining experience and make your culinary creations even more memorable.

This chapter is all about encouraging you to think outside the box and let your culinary creativity shine. Paw-paw leaves are a versatile ingredient that can be used in countless ways, so don't hesitate to try new combinations, experiment with flavors, and present your dishes in a way that makes your meals not only delicious but also visually stunning. The world of culinary exploration with paw-paw leaves is vast, and it's up to you to discover its full potential. Happy cooking!

Chapter 11: Caring for Paw-Paw Trees

If you're passionate about cooking with paw-paw leaves, it's essential to understand how to care for the paw-paw trees themselves. These trees are relatively easy to cultivate, but they do require specific care to thrive and provide you with an abundant supply of leaves for your culinary adventures.

Choosing the Right Location

Paw-paw trees thrive in well-drained soil and typically prefer partial shade to full sun. When planting your paw-paw tree, choose a location that offers these conditions. It's also essential to consider protection from strong winds, as the tree's leaves can be sensitive to windburn.

Soil Preparation

Before planting your paw-paw tree, it's a good idea to conduct a soil test. Paw-paw trees prefer slightly acidic soil with a pH between 5.5 and 7.0. You may need to amend the soil with organic matter or other amendments to create the right conditions for your tree to flourish.

Planting

Plant your paw-paw tree during the dormant season, either in late winter or early spring. The tree should be planted at the same depth as it was in the nursery container. Ensure proper spacing (typically 8-10 feet between trees) to allow for healthy growth.

Watering

Paw-paw trees need consistent moisture, especially during their first few years of growth. Water your tree regularly, keeping the soil consistently moist but not waterlogged. Be mindful of drought conditions, as paw-paw trees are sensitive to drought stress.

Pruning

Pruning helps to maintain the shape and size of your paw-paw tree, ensuring that it doesn't become overcrowded or too tall. Prune during the dormant season to remove dead or diseased branches and promote a healthy structure.

Fertilization

Paw-paw trees benefit from annual fertilization, typically in the spring. Use a balanced fertilizer with micronutrients, and follow the application instructions provided on the product. Avoid over-fertilization, as this can harm the tree.

Pest and Disease Management

Keep an eye out for common pests and diseases that can affect paw-paw trees, such as paw-paw zebra caterpillars or fungal issues. Regular inspections can help you catch and address these problems early.

Patience and Care

It's essential to remember that paw-paw trees may not produce leaves for culinary use until they are a few years old. Be patient and attentive to their care during this time, as healthy trees will eventually provide you with a consistent supply of leaves for your kitchen.

By understanding and following these guidelines for caring for your paw-paw trees, you can ensure they remain healthy and productive. With the right conditions and proper maintenance, you'll have an abundant source of paw-paw leaves to continue exploring and experimenting with unique culinary creations for years to come.

Conclusion: Embracing the Bounty of Paw-Paw Leaves

In the culinary journey we've embarked upon, we've explored the incredible world of paw-paw leaves – a unique and versatile ingredient that has been used for generations in various cultures. From its distinct flavor to its nutritional richness, paw-paw leaves have offered us a wealth of possibilities in the kitchen.

Throughout this guide, we've delved into traditional recipes, and adaptations for different diets, and even encouraged creative experimentation. We've discovered that paw-paw leaves can infuse a subtle, slightly nutty taste into a wide range of dishes, from soups and stews to snacks, desserts, and more. We've learned that these leaves are not only flavorful but also packed with essential vitamins and nutrients, making them a wonderful addition to a health-conscious kitchen.

As we close this culinary exploration, remember that the

journey doesn't have to end here. The world of cooking with paw-paw leaves is vast and full of potential. With a bit of creativity, you can continue to craft unique dishes that both surprise and delight your taste buds. Whether you're embracing a vegan lifestyle, seeking gluten-free options, or exploring keto-friendly recipes, paw-paw leaves offer the versatility to cater to your dietary preferences.

Furthermore, caring for your paw-paw trees allows you to have a consistent and sustainable supply of fresh leaves at your disposal. By providing the right conditions, such as well-drained soil and proper pruning, you can ensure your trees thrive and provide you with the key ingredients for your culinary adventures.

So, in the spirit of culinary exploration, we encourage you to continue your journey with paw-paw leaves. Experiment, innovate, and savor the unique essence they bring to your dishes. Share your creations with friends and family, and let the world discover the delightful and nutritious flavors of paw-paw leaves.

Thank you for joining us on this culinary adventure. May your kitchen continue to be a place of creativity, discovery, and, above all, delicious joy.

Printed in Great Britain
by Amazon

37496778R00056